Che Boludo!

A gringo's guide to understanding the Argentines

Che Boludo!

A gringo's guide to understanding the Argentines

James Bracken

Dibujos: Martín Chirulo

 EDITORIAL CALEUCHE

 **Ediciones Continente**

Bracken, James
    Che boludo / James Bracken ; edición a cargo de: Raúl Izaguirre
    1a ed. - Bariloche : Caleuche, 2005.

    ISBN 978-987-21731-2-8

    1. Jerga Argentina-Diccionario. I. Izaguirre, Raúl, ed. lit. II. Título
    CDD 467.982

Fecha de catalogación: 13/05/2005

¡Che Boludo!
1ª edición 2005
2ª edición 2007
James Bracken
shredgarr@hotmail.com

© Editorial Caleuche
C.C. 1728 (8400) Bariloche - Tel. (02944) 461478
www.patagonialibros.com.ar - rizaguirre@infovia.com.ar
Director Editorial: Raúl Izaguirre

Edición especial de 2000 ejemplares en exclusiva para
Ediciones Continente
Pavón 2229 (C1248AAE) Buenos Aires, Argentina
Tel.: (54-11) 4308-3535 - Fax: (54-11) 4308-4800
e-mail: info@edicontinente.com.ar
www.edicontinente.com.ar

Diseño de cubierta e interior: Nicolás Lai
Dibujos de tapa e interior: Martín Chirulo

Tengo que decir… muchísimas gracias a Alicia y Kevin por prestarme las máquinas. Muy buena onda! También, un abrazo fuerte al Capitán, Gabi, Tomás, Nico, Silvia, Gatito, mis viejos, el clan Frey y locos patagónicos. Todos son "re aparatos" y los quiero mucho! Gracias Martin por los dibujos buenísimos….y Bariloche, flashero!… y vos, corazón de arroz, la maestra más hermosa en el planeta. Tu paciencia no tiene fondo y no lo podría haber hecho sin vos.

Jaime

Prólogo

Argentines love to talk. They communicate directly, openly and often loudly. In Argentina there is no taboo in the use of foul language. A respectable old woman will swear like a sailor and no one bats an eye. Fools are not suffered lightly and anyone behaving in a pretentious or obnoxious manner will be sharply reprimanded, sometimes with just a simple gesture of the hands. Political correctness does not exist in Argentina because it would only impede getting your point across. If you are a little overweight your nickname might be 'el Gordo', or if you have a dark complexion they might call you 'Negro' or if you happen to be of Polish descent, 'el Polaco'. No offense is intended, none is taken and there is no false morality to confuse the issues. It is evident when Argentines communicate with one another that their freedom of speech is real. Although Argentines are extremely patriotic and will not hesitate to tell you that their country has the tallest mountains, the tastiest beef, the most beautiful women, the finest wine and the best soccer players in the world, they will also be quick to point out that their country is run by corrupt polititians and is full of bullshitters and crooks. The truth is "which country isn't?", but Argentines in particular always seem to be just as aware of their own shortcomings as well as they are of other's. This keen sense of discernment is illustrated by the vast quantity of words used to accurately describe an idiot, a braggart, a liar, a scam or the quality of anything from personal character to household appliances. The Argentines use these words with such frequency and passion that the unsuspecting foreigner will eventually have to ask "what is a 'boludo' and why can't I find it in my Spanish dictionary?"

The unique form of Spanish spoken in most of Argentina today is most accurately called Rio Platense. Rio Platense is commonly identified by its use of the pronoun 'vos' instead of 'tu' or 'usted' as well as a shh or a soft jj sound when pronouncing ll or y (eg. pollo-*posho*, yerba-*sherba*). Rio Platense is named for the Rio Plata which, as it drains into the Atlantic Ocean, borders the province of Buenos Aires and defines the most populated part of Argentina. Uruguay is located on the other side of the Rio Plata from Argentina and is also home to Rio Platense Spanish. Although geographically a massive country with an incredibly diverse population, Rio Platense has had the strongest cultural and lingual influences in most of Argentina due soley to the sheer number of those who speak it. The majority of this population is descended from the huge influx of immigrants that arrived, from all parts of the world, to the port of Buenos Aires in the early 20th century. The particular language and slang that evolved in the streets of Buenos Aires at this time is referred to as Lunfardo and is directly related to Tango music and culture. Lunfardo has its own vocabulary and word play such as syllable inversions (pizza – zapi, cafe-feca) that some say originated as a way for folks to communicate beyond the understanding of the police and prison guards. Much Lunfardo reflects a life of crime and could be why most Argentines appear to be so streetwise when speaking their native tongue. Although a great deal of Lunfardo has found a permanent place in the Argentine vocabulary, "Che Boludo!" is not a dictionary of Lunfardo but a comprehensive guide to understanding the slang, expressions, gestures and Rio Platense Spanish that is used throughout most of Argentina today. Everyone from the celebrated Tango singers to the infamous gauchos to the youth of today has made their contributions. Many words and expressions vary from province to province and person to person. To cover them all would be impossible as language is constantly crossing borders and evolving through the generations. In any case, it is important that this book is used wisely and you are among good friends before you go spouting out its contents. Certain colloquialisms are only appropriate in certain situations and a failure of good judgment could likely result in embarrassing yourself or, worse yet, offending someone and promptly receiving a trompada.

"Vos"

With the exception of a few other specific parts of Colombia, Bolivia and Central America, Rio Platense is unique in its use of the pronoun **'vos'** (you). Whether or not **'vos'** comes from Portuguese 'vôce', from Español **'vosotros'** or an antiquated form of addressing someone of the uptmost importance such as god or the king, its place in Rio Platense is accepted, by those who speak it, as legitimate Castellano. In Rio Platense, **'vos'** also has its own form of conjugation. The only differences between the conjugation of **'vos'** and **'tu'** are found in the simple present tense and imperative form and are usually only a matter of an accented syllable. If you speak using **'vos'** instead of **'tu'** or **'usted'**, however, it is important that you recognize these conjugations and use them accordingly. The examples given are to illustrate the differences between conjugating **'tu'** and **'vos'**. Rio Platense, like common Spanish, also uses **'usted'** in cases where respect is shown such as when speaking to an elderly with whom one is not intimate.

verb	vos	tu	imperative vos
ser (to be)	vos sos	tu eres	se!
estar (to be)	vos estás	tu estás	está!
caminar (to walk)	vos caminás	tu caminas	caminá!
tener (to have)	vos tenés	tu tienes	tené!
querer (to want)	vos querés	tu quieres	queré!
subir (to go up)	vos subís	tu subes	subí!
venir (to come)	vos venís	tu vienes	vení!
pensar (to think)	vos pensás	tu piensas	pensá!
decir (to say)	vos decís	tu dices	decí!
contar (to tell, to count)	vos contás	tu cuentas	contá!

DICCIONARIO

[m] masculine noun
[f] feminine noun
[v] verb
[adj] adjective
[antiquated] used by older generations
[excl] exclamation
[aug] augmented
[dim] diminutive
lit. literal meaning of the word

abrochar [v] lit. to button up; to fuck (vulgar)

abollado [adj] lit. dented; someone who appears to be in
    rough shape or abused

achaparrada [adj] short and stubby, used to describe
    vegetation

afanar [v] to steal, to rob; to over charge; to win by a
    large difference

alcahuete [m] Arabic in origin, from al-qawwd which means 'word'; 1) narc, informer to police; 2) tattle tale; someone not to be trusted with a secret 3) [antiquated] pimp; **alcahuetear** [v] to betray a secret, to be a tattle tale

amarrete [m] a haggler, a cheapskate

aparato [m] lit. apparatus; a real character of a person; a strange, eccentric person

apolillar [v] to sleep. *from a **polilla** [moth] sleeping in the cocoon

atorrante [m] 1) someone who is worthless, a lazy bum *this term originated in the early part of the century when large drain pipes, manufactured by the company Torrant, were used by the homeless as a place to sleep; 2) sometimes used affectionately for men or children; 3) a whorish woman

baboso/a [adj] drooling; used to describe someone who is lusty, with sexual desire 'very horny' **babosear** [v] to drool with desire

bacán [adj] someone with expensive tastes, who lives luxuriously and enjoys the finer things in life

baqueteado [adj] lit. a reamed musket; worn out, used to the point of disrepair

bagayo [m] 1) an ugly person, a dog of a woman; 2) baggage, luggage

bajón [m] lit. a decline, a drop; 'a downer',
    a disappointment or a bummer

banana [f] someone who thinks they are really cool but
    is never taken seriously by others

bancar [v] 1) to tolerate, to bear, to accept 2) to support,
    to help; to support financially

baranda [f] lit. a railing; a stench, a foul smell

bárbaro/a [adj, excl] 1) excellent, great;
    2) "que bárbaro!" 'wow!'

bardo [m] chaos; a crazy, annoying or problematic
    situation. **bardear** [v] "to make a bardo" to cause
    trouble

barullo [m] a noisy disuption

bicho [m] lit. a bug, a small animal, a 'critter'. **"mal
    bicho"** 'bad bug' used in reference to Argentina's
    corrupt politicians

bife [m] lit. a beefsteak; a slap in the face

birra [f] {Italian} beer

bizarro/a [m,f] bizarre, strange

bocha [f] a large quantity of something

bocho/a [m,f] smart, quick witted

bola [f]   lit. ball;   testical   *also **"dar bola"** 'to give the ball' to pay attention to; eg. **"no me dan bola"** 'they don't give me the ball' they don't pay attention to me *this probably comes from soccer, the number one sport in Argentina also: **"romper las bolas"** 'to break one's balls' **"hinchar las bolas"** 'to swell one's balls' to be annoying, a pain in the ass **"en bolas"** 'to be in balls' to be naked; to be in a bad situation without protection, as if you were naked and exposed

"no me dan bola"

bolazo[m] a gross lie or exaggeration

boleado [adj] to be dizzy

boleta [f] lit. a receipt; a lie

boleto [m] lit. a ticket (bus, plane, etc.)
   "sos boleto" 'you're dead'

bólido [m] an automobile

bolita [f] derogatory for a Bolivian

boludo/a [m,f] lit. one with large testicles but not used
   to describe someone who is brave or 'ballsy'; used
   alike for men, women and children; 1) fool, idiot;
   2) same definition but also used casually among
   friends thus **"che boludo!"** could be anything
   from 'you idiot!' to 'hey buddy' depending on the
   context of the situation *historical fact: **"boludos"**
   or **"pelotudos"** were 'cannon fodder', the first
   troops to be sent into battle and thus the first to be
   killed *see: **pelotudo**
   "hacerse el boludo" [v] to play dumb, to act as if
   you don´t know
   boludez [f] any matter easy to solve, something
   that can be done by any boludo
   buenudo/a [adj] someone who is kind of dumb or
   naive but a good person

bombacha [f] a traditionally baggy pants worn by the
   Argentine gauchos; **bombacha** is now more
   commonly used for women's panties
   chabomba [lunfardo]

bombo [m]   lit. a big drum;   an unexpected and/or undesired pregnancy, a big belly

bombón [m,f] lit. candy, usually chocolate; hey gorgeous!, an attractive man or woman

bondi [m]   public bus   * this word comes from the English 'bonds' that were used to fund the installation of the famous trams, called 'bondes', of Rio de Janeiro, Brazil

bonete [m] lit. a pointed hat **"del bonete"** crazy

bosta [f]   horseshit; someone or something that is very ugly

borrego [m] a kid *see: **pibe**

botón [m,f]   lit. a button; a tattle tale [antiq.] police; informer to the police *see: **buchón**

brasuca [adj] a Brazilian; sometimes derogatory

brutal [adj, excl]   lit. brutal; great, awesome; 'wow!'

buchón [m]   a tattle tale; an informer to police, 'narc' *see: **alcahuete**

bulín [m] lit. lathe used in a plaster wall; a room or place used to have sex

bulto [m] lit. package; penis and testicals

buzarda [f] a big belly

cábala [f] a gesture that brings good luck, eg. An old Italian tradition still observed by older generations in Argentina, is to eat gnoccis on the 29th of every month. It is a **cábala** to put coins under the plates of the gnoccis

caber [v] lit. to fit into; to like someone, to get along well with someone, eg. **"me cabe el chabón"** 'I really like that guy'

cachengue [m] a great party, usually with good music and lots of dancing

cacho [m] a piece or chunk of something **"un cacho de carne con ojos"** 'a piece of meat with eyes' an idiot; [dim] **"cachito"** a small quantity of something "a tiny bit"

cachucha [f] a vagina

cachuso/a [adj] something or someone that functions poorly or is flawed

cagar [v] lit. to shit; to wreck, ruin or fall apart; to screw someone over **garca** [lunfardo] someone who screws people over

cagarse [v] to break down, to fall apart also: **"estar cagado"** lit. 'to be shitted'; to have big problems, to be fucked
"cagar a palos" lit. 'to shit to the sticks'; to beat the shit out of

"cuiqui"
'to be afraid'

"cagar la fruta" lit. shit the fruit; to die; **"tener un cagaso"** lit. to have a huge shit; to be very scared

"cagón" lit. big shit; a coward

"caga de risa" lit. a shit of laughter; hilarious

"cagar de frio" lit. to shit from cold; to be freezing your ass off

cana [f] 1) police: 2) jail

canchero [m] a smooth talker, a know it all *from **"cancha"** the horse tracks, a canchero would be someone who knows "the tracks" thus which horse to bet on

caño [m] lit. a pipe, a tube; 1) pipe used to smoke marijuana or also marijuana cigarette; a joint; 2) **"dar con un caño"** lit. 'hit with a pipe'; to deal someone a heavy verbal blow, to publicly criticize or denounce someone such as a polititian; 3) a pistol

canuto/a [adj] originally a lock pick used by thieves, something hidden **encanutar** [v] to hide something, generally illicit

capo/a [m,f] 1) a popular person, someone who is well liked due to a generous nature; 2) boss, chief, someone that has control on the situation

careta [adj] lit. 'wearing a mask'; pretentious, snobbish; used to describe fashion conscious people or expensive restaurants and neighborhoods [aug] **caretón**

21

caretear [v] to act falsely

carucha [adj] a good looking person

cascote [adj] lit. a piece of stone; someone who is hard headed thus slow to learn

catrasca [f] **"cagada tras cagada"** lit. 'one shit after another'; one disaster after another; a klutz

catrera [f] a bed

cebar [v] lit. to choke the carburetor of an auto; to serve mates. *see: **mate culture**

cepillar [v] lit. to brush; to fuck (vulgar)

chabón [m] guy, man

chacota [phrase] **"a la chacota"**   'slapped together' put together in haste

chamuyero [m] a smooth talker, a bullshitter, a know it all, someone with the characteristics of a used car salesman; **chamuyar** [v] to bullshit, to smooth talk somebody

chanfleado [adj] bent, curved; from the curve ball effect sometimes used when kicking the soccer ball

changa [f] temporary work, an 'odd job'

"la posta"
'without question, the absolute best'

changüi [m] a needed advantage or opportunity;
 'a break' eg. **"dame un changüi"** 'give me a
 break'

chanta [f] a smooth talker, a liar, someone who talks
 shit

chantajear [v] to be a chanta *see: **chamuyero**

chapa [f] lit. sheet or flat piece of metal **"a las chapas"**
 to go very fast

chata [f] lit. a bed pan; 1) pickup truck or van;
 2) a boring person

che [exl]   1) hey!, hey you! 2) also used as a
 meaningless interjection in whatever context
 *The origins of this catchy expletive are debated.
 The most popular theory is that che comes from
 the Mapuzungun language spoken by the native
 Patagonian Mapuche. In Mapuzungun, **che** means
 'people'. **Che** also means 'I' in the language
 spoken by the Guaraní, natives of the Paraná River
 basin of northern Argentina. Considering the roots
 of Rio Platense, **che** could also come from 'tse',
 an old Spanish expletive used to get someone's
 attention or tell them to 'shut up' or the Italian
 'che' which in Spanish would be **'hay'** (there are)
 * It is also to be understood that che was not
 adopted into Argentine vocabulary from Argentine
 revolutionary hero Ernesto 'Che' Guevara. Che
 Guevara received his nickname because the
 Argentine's frequent use of **'che'** often distinguishes
 them from other Latin Americans

cheto/a [adj] fancy, expensive, wealthy

china [f] a gaucho's woman

chinchudo/a [adj] nervous, hysterical, short tempered

chirimbolo [m] random objects, watchamacallits;
    see: **huevadas**

chirimbolear [v] to fix something accordingly with
    creativity and whatever is at hand, 'jerry rig'

chirola [f] spare change

chocho/a [adj] [antiq] ok!, great, happy, satisfied

chorro/a [m,f] a crook, a thief, a suspicious character

chorongo/a [adj] of poor quality, shitty

choto/a [m,f;adj] penis; of bad quality, shitty

chuchi [adj] a heavily groomed woman; lots of makeup,
    big hair, long, painted fingernails, poodle with a
    ribbon, etc.

chumbo [m] a pistol

chupamedias [m,f] lit. a sock sucker; ass kisser, brown
    noser, boot licker

chupar [v] lit. to suck; to drink alcohol, generally in
    large quantities

"coger"

ciruja [f] a beggar, a bum

coger [v] lit. to grab, to get, to collect; to fuck

colgarse [v] lit. to hang one's self; to be spaced out, to be flaky or a slacker; to hang out and do nothing; to concentrate heavily on something

comerse [v] lit. to eat; used to describe one's involvement in a situation, generally with negative connotations such as: **"comerse una pelicula"** 'to eat yourself a film'; to be involved in a complicated situation, generally negative **"comerse la cabeza"** 'to eat your head'; to be worried or have problems

concha [f] lit. shell; vagina, pussy, cunt
    conchuda [f] a cunt of a woman; common expressions **"la concha de tu madre!"** 'your mother's pussy' **"la concha de la lora"** 'the parrot's pussy' (in the old days prostitutes were called **'loras'**) these are used as general insults or exclamations such as 'goddammit!'
    [lunfardo] **chacón**

copado/a [adj] a cool friendly person; anything that is cool or agreeable

cotorra [f] lit. parakeet; vagina, pussy **"picar la cotorra"** lit. to have an itchy parakeet; when a woman is sexually stimulated or horny

corchito/a [m,f] lit. a little cork; a short person

cortado [m] a coffee expresso with a shot of milk

cosa [f] lit. thing; used as 'watchamacallit' or 'whats-his-name, whats-her-name'

cornudo/a [adj] lit. to have horns; used for someone who's partner is sleeping around on them, also used as heavy insult

crepar [v] to die, to pass away

cualquiera [exl; adj] lit. whatever; used to describe someone or something that is not to be taken seriously, kind of ridiculous

cuero [m] lit. leather **'sacar el cuero'** to talk badly behind someone's back, to gossip

culo [m] ass, buttocks [phrase] **"que culo!"** 'what luck!'

culiado [m] reciever of anal sex; used as an expletive, as an insult or among friends to address one another

curro [m] a scam or fraud;
    currar [v] to scam; to earn big by working little, often in reference to politicians

cursi [adj] in bad taste, cheap, generally refers to women

curtir [v] lit. to tan hide into leather; 1) to use accordingly, to settle into a good situation or place; 2) to date or sleep with someone; 3) to steal

denso/a [adj] lit. dense, thick; someone who is boring to the point of being annoying

deriva [adj] lit. to be adrift **"a la deriva"** to be wandering, without direction; usually implies a state of happiness

"un cortado"

desaparecidos [m] the disappeared ones; This refers to the victims of past military regimes in Argentina. The most recent and horrific period of human rights violations occured between the years of 1976-1983 in which more than thirty thousand students, intellectuals and activists were kidnapped, tortured and mudered. These desaparecidos are far from forgotten and many of their families currently continue seeking their justice.

despelote [m] a mess, disorder; see: quilombo

dibujado [adj] lit. to be drawn, to be painted; to be in a foreign situation or out of your element, to be visibly stoned from smoking pot also: **pintado** (painted)

diego [m] ten pesos worth of marijuana, 'dime bag'

embole [m] something that is very boring

engancharse [v] lit. to hook yourself; to get wrapped up in a situation

enroscar [v] lit. to screw; 1) to be confused, to have problems, to have 'issues'; 2) to be caught up in a situation

ensillar [v] to saddle up; to change the yerba in the mate when it begins to taste diluted, often just a portion of the yerba is changed *see: **mate culture**

escabiar [v] to intoxicate with alcohol

falopa [f] drugs

falopera /o [f,m] a drug addict

fanfarrón /a [m,f] smooth talker; know it all

faso [m] 1) [antiq.] cigarette; 2) marijuana

fiaca [f] tiredness, laziness; to have fiaca is to feel like doing nothing at all

fiambre [m] lit. cold cuts of meat; a dead body

fifar [v] to fuck (vulgar)

fija [adj] an absolute truth; [excl.] absolutlely!

fisurado/a [adj] exhausted, dead tired

flash [exl] cool!, awesome! **flashearse** [v] to blow ones mind, usually in a positive sense

forro [f] lit. protective cover; 1) condom, prophylactic 2) asshole of a person

franelear [v] lit. to polish with a flannel cloth; to kiss, to caress, a show of affection between lovers

full [adj] {English} **'a full'** to be very busy, to be engrossed in something, to be complete; also used like 'totally' or 'fully'

31

galán [m]   winner, ladies man

gamba [f] {Italian} leg; **"meter la gamba"** 'to put in the leg' to make a mistake, to screw up a situation **"hacer la gamba"** to help someone out

garcha [f] something that really sucks; from **garchar** [v] to fuck (vulgar)

Gardel [n] lit. famous singer who brought Tango from the underground to the mainstream; the best, **"Sos Gardel!"** 'You're the man!'

garrón [m] a bummer, a pain in the ass

gatillar [v] lit. to pull the trigger; to pay the bill, to spend money rapidly

gil [m] an idiot; **"gil de goma"** a complete idiot

guampudo/a [adj] to have horns;   *see: **cornudo**

grasa [f] lit. grease; cheesy, of poor taste and quality

groncho/a [adj] 1) derogatory for negro; 2) cheesy

groso [m] {Portuguese} lit. large; an important person, someone outstanding their field eg. **"Mick Jagger es un groso!"**

guacho/a [m,f] lit. orphan; 1) son of a bitch; 2) also used affectionately **"que guacho!"** 'that rascal!'

langa [lunfardo] someone who thinks they are a ladies man but is really a fool

guarango/a [adj]   gross, disgusting

guaso /a [m,f]   a rude and tasteless person

guita [f]   money, cash

guitarrear [v]   lit. to play the guitar; to talk in circles, never getting to the point

gula [f]   lit. greed, gluttony; extreme hunger resulting from smoking marijuana, 'the munchies'

hecha mierda [phrase]   lit. made of shit; broken, fucked up, screwed, exhausted, depressed or general bad state *also **"hecha percha"** lit. 'made like a coat hanger'

hostia [f]   lit. sacrificial victim; the wafer eaten as the body of christ; of huge or excessive proportions

huevos [m]   lit. eggs; testicals
        *also **huevón/a** [m] fool, idiot; see: **boludo**;
        huevada [f] a random and useless object

jamón! [exl]   'what a beautiful woman!'

joya! [excl]   lit. gem, jewel; excellent, great!, OK!

laburar [v] {Italian}   to work

lacra [f]   scum, bottom feeder, lowlife; refers to the character of a person rather than financial or social standing

lastrar [v] to eat

larva [f] larva; worthlessly lazy, someone who does nothing

lavado [adj] lit. washed; used to describe the state of the mate when the **yerba** has become diluted and no longer desirable *see: **mate culture**

lenteja [adj] lit. lentil; slow *from **lento** [lunfardo] **jalente**

lienzo [m] pants

lija [f] lit. sandpaper; hunger **"tengo una lija terrible!"** 'I'm starving!'

limado/a [adj] lit. filed, dulled; someone who is burned out or slow witted, usually from excessive drug use

locachi [adj] a bit crazy; from **loco**

lompa [f] pants

lomo [m] lit. a cut of beef, loin; used to describe a nice body

luca [f] an amount of one thousand, usually money

lungo/a [adj] a tall and thin person; lanky; also **"hacer lungo"** to be annoyingly slow

macana [f] a mistake, an error *also: **"que macana!"** 'what a shame'

macanudo/a [adj, excl] [antiquated] 1) someone agreeable, a friendly person; 2) 'sounds good' positive response to an deal or arrangement

machazo [adj] 1) large, huge; 2) very masculine, macho

malco [m] from **"mal cogido"** 'badly fucked' used for someone who is in a bad mood assuming because they are not getting laid properly

mamarse [v] lit. to breastfeed; to get very drunk
mamado/a [adj] to be drunk

mambo [m] lit. African rhythms used in Latin American music; used to describe someone or something with bad vibes, issues or problems; an undesired situation

mamerto /a [m,f] a complete idiot

manducar [v] to eat quickly, to wolf down food

manguear [v] to ask for money
manguero [n] someone who always asks for something, a mooch

mango [m] lit. a handle; a tropical fruit; 1) a peso unit; eg **"diez mangos'** ten pesos; 2) **"al mango"** full volume, full speed

masa [f] lit.dough; awesome, terrific

"tomando unos mates"

Mate Culture

Mate is THE traditional beverage of Argentina. For the Argentines, **'los mates'** are a fundamental part of life. **Mate** is a strong, caffeinated tea drank from a hollow guourd about the size of an apple. The guourd is filled with an herb and hot water and then drank through a metal straw called **'la bombilla'** that has a filter on the end. **Mates** can be fashioned out of anything from wood to a bull's horn and intricately ornated with silver and traditional carvings, a common guourd or small metal cup is more commonly used. Upon first glance, a mate session can appear to be some sort of tribal drug ritual and a few uninformed gringos have even been known to try to ignite and smoke the contents of the mate when passed their way. **Mates**, like coffee or tea in most other countries, are drank in the morning to help wake up as well as anytime of the day between friends who want to relax and speak frankly about matters. It must first be made clear that **mate** is the drink itself as well as the gourd it is drunk from. The actual herb placed inside the mate is **yerba**. Not hierba nor mate, but **yerba** or **yerba mate**. This **yerba** is grown in the northern, warmer and more fertile provinces of Argentina such as Corrientes and Misiones. Mate customs vary from person to person and place to place but some fundamental practices are important. There is one server **(cebador)** who must take charge of serving the **mates**. It is traditionally the chore of the youngest person present to serve the elders the mates. The server must begin by heating the water in the kettle **(pava)** and filling the mate with an appropriate portion of **yerba**. It is important that the water does not reach a boil. Most experts agree that 82 C is optimal.

Once the water is properly heated the server will pour himself the first as to be sure it is suitable for consumption. Sometimes the server will spit out the first few as they tend to be quite bitter. Some servers will place a spoonful of sugar in the mate to curb the bitterness and sweeten the **yerba**, this depends on the personal tastes of those drinking the mates. The **mate** is then passed from person to person. Each person drinks the entire contents of the mate and passes it back to the server who refills the mate and passes it to the next. Often the yerba will become diluted or 'washed' (**lavado**) before the kettle is empty and it will be necessary to change a portion (**ensillar**) or all of the yerba in the mate. When the kettle is drained the entire process is repeated and continues on until the last person decides that he or she has drunk enough mates. This can sometimes last the good part of a day. Serving mates is a big resonsibility and it is important that the server is attentive to the quality of the mates as well as the continuity and fluidity of their service. One will be sharply reminded that the mate **'no es un microfono!'** if he or she hangs on to it for too long while prophetilizing about this or that. **Mate** is serious business in Argentina.

milonga [f] a type of Tango with a faster beat

mina [f] [lunfardo] a lady; lacks respect

minga! [excl] no way!, of course not!, fuck you!

mocazo [m] lit. a large snot; 1) a big mistake;
      2) sometimes used to adress children

morfa [f] food; **morfar** [v] to eat

morocho/a [adj] someone with dark hair and complexion; **'moreno'** in common Spanish

morondanga [f] [antiq] worthless objects, anything of poor quality

mosca [f] lit. mosquito; money, cash

mufa [f] bad luck, a bad omen

mozzarella! [exl] 'quiet, don't say a word!' This incongruous exclamation comes from a secret code once used by an Agentine president to silence a reporter who was writing unsavory things about the government

nabo /a [m,f] lit. a raddish; an idiot, a fool

napia [f] the nose

ñoqui [m] lit. gnocci; someone who earns money without working, on the job but worthless *this popular term came into use after the discovery of false government salaries that had been arranged by workers who did nothing but collect the checks. These checks were received on the 29th of every month, the same day that gnoccis are traditionally eaten

ojete [m] 1) ass; 2) good luck *see: **orto**

onda [f] lit. waves, vibes eg. **micro onda** 'microwave'; somebody or something with **"buena onda"** would be really cool and with good vibes; to do something **'de onda'** 'is to do someone a favor; **'tirar una onda'** is to help somebody out

orto [m] ass, buttocks; 1) **"que orto!"** 'what good luck!' or 'what a nice ass!' depending on the context; 2) **"cara de orto"** lit. 'ass face', a sour face; 3) **"a la loma del orto"** lit. 'the hill of the ass' the middle of nowhere

pachanguear [v] to party; **pachanga** [f] a fiesta

pachorra [f] laziness, to feel like doing nothing

pajero/a [m,f] a jackoff ; from **"hacer la paja"** lit. to make straw; to masturbate

pajerto/a [m,f] an idiot

palo [m] lit. stick **"al palo"** 'to the stick', to have an erection

palo verde [m] lit. a green stick; million dollars

papear [v] 1) to talk shit; 2) to eat

papelón [m] an embarrassing situation

parir [v] lit. to give birth; to struggle incredibly as if giving birth

patovica [m] a weight lifter, body guard or bouncer

pava [f] kettle   * see: **mate culture**

pedigüeño/a [m,f] someone who is always asking for something, a mooch

pedo [m] lit. a fart; *common expressions 1) **'cagar a pedos'** lit.'to shit farts', to scold, to berate; 2) **'al pedo'** for nothing, a waste of time, money or energy; 3) **'en pedo'** lit. 'in farted', to be intoxicated, to be drunk **'ni en pedo'** 'no way', 'not even if I was drunk'; 4) **'de pedo'** by chance; 5) **'a los pedos'** lit. to the farts to go very fast; 6) **pedorro** lit. 'farty', shitty, of poor quality

la vida regida por los pedos - life ruled by farts

0-20 años	se vive al pedo
20-40 años	se vive a los pedos
40-60 años	se vive en pedo
60-80 años	se vive de pedo
80-100 años	ni en pedo!

*also: **'pedo con caldo'** lit. 'fart with broth' to follow through on a fart, to 'draw mud'

película [f] lit. a film; a problematic, annoying or amusing situation

pelota [f] a ball **"dar pelota"** lit. 'give the ball'; to pay attention to **'hinchar las pelotas'** lit. to swell one's balls; to bother or annoy, to be a 'pain in the ass'.

"no me hinchés las pelotas"

pelotudo/a [m,f] lit. one with big balls; idiot or fool.
  *see: **boludo**

peluca [f] lit. a wig; cottonmouth received from smoking
  pot, as if you had a wig in your mouth

pendejo /a [m,f] a pubic hair; an adolescent, a youth
  *also: **pendevieja** [f] from pendejo; an older
  woman who tries to keep up with youthful
  fashions

pepa [f] a pill; a hit of LSD

pesado/a [adj] lit. heavy; boring, annoying

pescado/a [m,f] lit. fish; an idiot

pesto [m] wind, rain, snow, threatening weather

petar [v] to fall apart physically or mentally;
  petado [adj] in a bad state *see: **hecho mierda**

pibe/a [m,f] a kid, a guy

pifiar [v] to make a big mistake **"pifiaste!"** 'you really
  screwed up!'

pijotero/a [m,f] a cheapskate, a haggler

pilas [f] lit. batteries; this refers to the energy of a
  person, someone **"muy pilas"** would be motivated
  and positive **"ponete las pilas!"** 'put in your
  batteries!', get going! **"sacate las pilas"** 'take
  your batteries out!' chill out!, take it easy

pilcha [f] clothes

pintar [v]   lit. to paint;   to appear a situation or opportunity, to come up; pinta, appearance
"que pinta!" 'it looks good!'

piola [adj] 1) clever, intelligent; an agreeable person
2) **"quedarse piola"** to hang out and do nothing

pintado/a [adj] lit. painted; crazy

pipón [adj] to be full from overeating

pirar [v] to go crazy **pirado** [adj] to be crazy

pirucho/a [adj] crazy

piturrear [v] to smoke a joint

plomo [m] lit. lead; someone or something that is very boring

pocilga [f] a rat's hole, a dirty and disgusting place

pornoco [m]   a zit; from **"por no coger"** 'by not fucking' zits as if recieved due to a lack of sexual activity

poronga [f] a penis; someone or something that really sucks

porro [m] marijuana, a joint

porteño/a [m,f] lit. someone from the port; anyone from Buenos Aires

posta [excl.] the truth 'seriously!'

pucho [m] a cigarette

pro [adj] {English} from professional; something well done, in a professional manner

putear [v] from 'puta' 'whore'; to use foul language

querusa [adj] someone or something of lower quality, cheap, scruffy

quilombo [m] a mess, disorder, chaos *originally, quilombos were the slave's quarters in Brazil's sugar plantations. The brothels of Buenos Aires were also refered to as quilombos. also: **quilombero/a** [m,f] someone who creates quilombos, a troublemaker; **bolonqui** [lunfardo]

rajar [v] to crack, to tear; used like 'to split' eg. **"rajemos"** 'let's get out of here'

rascar [v] lit. to scratch; to do nothing at all **"rascar las bolas"** 'scratch your balls'

raviol [m] a small packet of cocaine

TAC
TAC

"tacaño"

rolinga [adj] Rolinga is in reference to the Rolling Stones and Argentina's rock and roll youth which strongly identifies with the Stones' flamboyant, badboy style. The Rolling Stone's trademark lips and extended tongue can be seen throughout Argentina on T-shirts, tatoos, stickers, and graffiti.

sacado/a [adj] lit. removed; intensly crazy, a state of insanity, as if all reason has been taken (**sacado**) from from your mind

salame [m] an idiot, a fool

sanata [f] an embellished and exagerrated story that is generally far from the truth

sopapo [m] a slap in the face

sorete [m] a turd, a log of shit

tacaño [m] a cheapskate, someone who always haggles for a bargain

taco [m] the high heel of a shoe; to do something '**al taco**' is to do it with ease and flair as a football player would score a goal with a touch of his heel

tano/a [m,f] an Italian

tapera [adj] 1) a modest house; 2) in ruins, abandoned.

tipo [m] [lufardo] a man, a guy

toque [m] lit. a touch; 'a little bit'; **"al toque"** quickly, instantly

tornillo [m] lit. screw; cold **"que tornillo barbaro!"** 'it's damn cold!'

tortillera [f] a lesbian, also: **torta** [f]

transar [v] 1) to french kiss; 2) to make an illegal deal or agreement

traste [m] ass

travesaño [m] a transvestite

trola [f] a promiscuos woman

trolo [m] a homosexual man

trompa [f] mouth **trompada** [f] a punch in the mouth

trucho/a [adj] lit. trout; fake, false, of poor quality

tubazo [m] a telephone call **tubo** [m] lit. a tube; 1) a telephone; 2) a big bicep

viste [exl.] past tense of the verb ver, 'did you see?'; used frequently like "you know?" or meaningless interjection

yapa [f] a monetary tip; **'de yapa'** besides, also

yuta [f] [antiq.] police

zafar [v] lit. to get away with something, to slip, to untie; to be acceptable, not great but okay

zafarrancho [m] a mess, disorder *see: **quilombo**

zarpar [v] lit. to weigh anchor and set sail; **zarparse** [v] to go beyond the norm or accepted limits; **zarpado** [adj] wild, mind blowing

zoquete [m] lit. short socks; an idiot, a fool

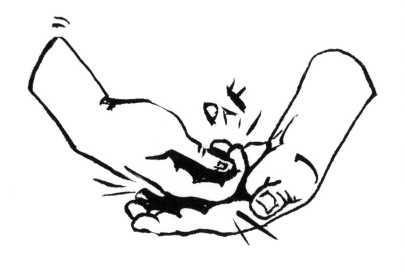

"¡hay que pagar!"
'you must pay'

Los Dichos

"a las chapas"   to go very fast.

"estar en el horno"   lit. to be in the oven; to be higly stressed or in a bad situation.

"me quema la cabeza"   lit. it burns my head; it makes me crazy, used mostly in the negative sense.

"tirar para arriba"   lit. to throw in the air; to have an excess of something.

"un pelo de la concha tira más que una yunta de bueyes"   'one pussy hair pulls more than a team of oxen'.

"echar un polvo"   lit. to throw a dust; to fuck.

"chiva como puto nuevo"   'sweat like a new fag'.

"renegué como puto nuevo" 'complain like a new fag'.

"tirar las chancletas"   lit. throw off the sandals; used for women who are on a sexual rampage.

"tirar la casa por la ventana"   'to throw the house out the window'; to go wild and out of control

"tirame la goma"   'pull my rubber'; suck my dick

"¿qué te pasa?"
'what's your problem?!'
'what's up with that?!'

"mojar la chaucha" 'to get the peapod wet'; to get laid

"meter la mula" 'to put in the the mule'; to trick someone, rip someone off

"echando putas" 'throwing out the whores'; to go very fast

"para atrás" 'to go backwards'; used for someone or something that is disfunctional.

"la sacaste barata" 'you got it cheap'; you got away with murder, it could have been worse.

"le faltan algunos jugadores" 'he's missing some players'; he's a bit crazy or dumb.

"lo atamos con alambre" 'we tie it with wire'; to jerry-rig it, to get the job done with whatever resources are at hand.

"hasta las manos" 'up to the hands'; to have your hands full *also **'hasta las bolas'**.

"calienta la pava pero no ceba los mates" 'he/she heats the kettle but doesn't serve the mates"; he/she's a prick tease

"al pedo como teta de monja" 'useless like tits on a nun' *see: **pedo**

"la noche está en pañales" 'the night is in diapers'; 'the night is young'

"marca cañón!" 'cannon brand'; used like 'totally'

"¡tomátela!"

"media naranja" 'half orange'; affectionate for one's lover, spouse or partner

"tomatelá!" 'take it'; get out of here!, fuck you!

"mandar fruta" 'to send fruit'; to lie, to talk shit *see: **chamuyar**

"caer como peludo de regalo" 'to fall like the gift of an armadillo'; a surprise visit by an undesired guest

"tener una vena" 'to have a vein' to be pissed off angry, as if the veins in your neck and head were showing

"ponerse la camiseta" 'to put on the jersy'; to be a team player or 'company guy'

"comerse un huesito" 'to eat a little bone'; to sleep with a beautiful woman

"hacer una vaquita" 'to make a little cow'; to put money in a communal pot

"no da" 'it doesn't give'; 1) unacceptable, 'that doesn't fly' 2) the opportunity is not given

"ni a ganchos!" 'not even by the hooks!'; no way!

"ni a palos!" 'not even by the sticks!'; no way!

"cerrado como culo de muñeca" 'closed like a doll's ass'

"¡ni idea!"

"que parte la tierra!" 'how the earth splits!' 'what a beautiful woman!', as if the earth parts beneath her feet

"moco de pavo" 'turkey snot'; something very easy to do

"hacerse la manuela" to masturbate

"no le llega agua al tanque" 'water doesn't get to his tank'; someone who is bit dim.

"te fuiste a la mierda" 'you went to the shit'; 'you've gone too far', 'you outdid yourself'.

"¡ojo!"
'be careful!'
'watch out for ...'

Gente

Argentines sometimes have interesting ways of greeting each other or refering to someone. These are often used affectionately refering to someone's appearance or in whatever context with no significance at all. They are not meant to be offensive and thus not taken personally.

cabeza	head (also derogatory for the poor)
cabezón	big head
chabón	guy
flaco/a	skinny
gordo	fatty
jefe	boss
loco/a	crazy
maestro	master
morocho/a	one with a dark complexion
negro/a	black one
papá	father
pelado	baldy
vieja	old woman (used by guys)
winner	winner

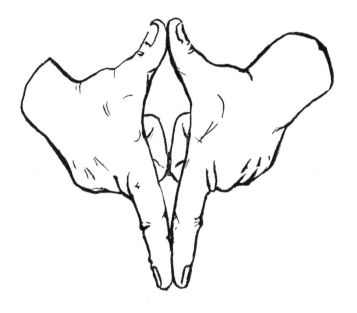

"la concha"

EDITORIAL CALEUCHE

Algunos Títulos Publicados
Crónica Histórica del Nahuel Huapi
Toponimia del Parque Nacional Nahuel Huapi
Diccionario Mapuche-Español
El Mate
Antártida: descubriendo el continente blanco
El Gran Lago
El Cabo Savino
Flora y Fauna Patagónicas
Mountain Bike en Bariloche
Las Montañas de Bariloche
Pescando Truchas
El Corredor de los Lagos Andino Patagónicos
Panes, pizzas y tartas
La Soja y el Tofu
Talasoterapia
Andinismo y Esquí

Guías
Patagonia 2005 (37a. edición)
Patagonia Austral
Patagonia: Corredor de las Playas
Salta
El Noroeste
La Rioja
Miniturismo
La Costa Verde Argentina
Pinamar y Villa Gesell
Playas Patagónicas
Rutas Argentino-Chilenas (Andino-Patagónicas)
Parque Nacional Los Glaciares
Mapa Patagonia